Sammy Spider's Rockwall

Story MADE in Canada

KidsBooksByNaila LLC

Library of Congress Copyright 2025

Far away in the depths of the RED rocky canyons, lived a spider named Sammy who looked upon the horizon.

Now Sammy you see was the size of a pea,
His black legs stretched out as long as could be.

One fine afternoon Sammy went out to go crawling, he climbed over the ledges without even stalling!
He suddenly came to a halt in his walk where he noticed a wall that was BIG, RED and ROCK!

He looked oh so closely to decide what to do...
he even wondered if maybe,
he could climb that wall too!

As he stared and he stared, he felt a little scared,
"that wall is too big", he said as he GLARED!
"Its time for me to turn back around, and crawl
under my big, round, dirt covered mound...

Sammy crawled back to his home in the dirt,
relieved that he now knew,
he COULD not get hurt.

As Sammy lay sleeping in the dirt by the wall, he had many dreams about that wall that stood tall.

He dreamed of how he could just climb up the pitch, then awoke as he fell to the ground, in a ditch.

As the morning came on and the Sun had now rose, Sammy headed out from his mound where he had gone in for a doze.

He travelled back to the wall to try it once more, but then he looked at it again and thought, "what a CHORE"!

WHAT A CHORE!!

He headed back to where he came from, with his head hung so low and his legs were all numb.

Sammy did not think he could make the big climb, so instead that FURRY black spider turned back and whined.

I can't climb over that rocky old wall, all the stones will come loose and upon me they'll fall!

Woahhhh!

Sammy crawled back to his little dirt house and he felt like he acted like a little scared mouse.

He wanted so badly to climb up that wall, though he wanted to do it without a hard fall!

The next day had come and
Sammy went crawling,
as he looked up
at the wall, it looked like
someone was falling.

He crawled even closer
to see what was
going on, he was hoping
they'd fall on
a fresh patch of lawn!

He looked up above and to his surprise,
was a girl that was dangling from
a rope ten feet high! He stared and he
wondered, "what was she doing"?
He watched
from afar,
all the flies
he kept
shoo-ing!

SHOO!

The next thing he saw was a guy on the wall,
he looked so lean, so trim and so tall!
He would place his hands and his feet right
into the holds, which are holes, ledges
and grabs, around your fingers can fold.

As he placed one of his feet, which he
SMEARED in the ledge,
he grabbed up with one hand in
the hold he did wedge.

One foot, one hand above one another, *carabiner*
then a big long red rope holding all of it together.

◁ ROPE

You see if the climber would slip and fall to the flats, the rope would then catch him so he didn't go SPLAT!
He also was using something big round and metal, it looked like a clamp, in the rock it did settle.
He would connect the big rope to the clamps and carabiners, Sammy knew he could do this or was he just a big dreamer??

SPLAT!

Sammy started to climb up the great red rock wall. He placed his legs one by one, one up and one down. Sammy no longer had that sad little frown.
He spun a big line from one hold to the next and he could not wait to get over that deck.
Halfway up he had still not fallen down,
He could not believe he could not hear a sound!

It was so very peaceful on that wall he did climb, he made his climb to the top, Sammy made it just fine!
As he sat at the top, he looked all the way yonder, he sat there in deep happy thoughts and did ponder.......

He knew he did not need the rope or the clamp, his spider's web would serve as an excellent ramp.

This spider's web ramp used to get to the top, then repelling back down it, maybe adding some hops!

Now Sammy is no longer scared of rock walls, he can get over anything and for sure with no falls.
Next time that anyone you know has a fear, tell them out loud so that they will hear, "conquer this friend without shedding a tear"!

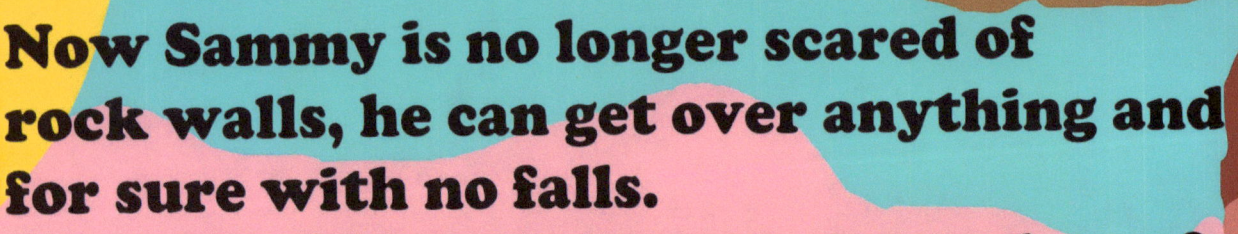

Kids Books By Naila

Out Now! More Stories to engage your adventurous spirit!

Coming soon

  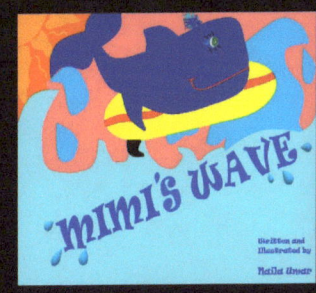 

Available on Amazon now!!

Available on paperback now at www.kidsbooksbynaila.com and www.kidsbooksbynaila.ca

www.ingramcontent.com/pod-product-compliance
Lightning Source LLC
Chambersburg PA
CBHW042129040426
42450CB00002B/126